# QUILTER'S
## NOTEBOOK II

Design and illustrations by Cheryl A. Benner

*"Our ancestors quilted what they knew: hardship and joy, birth and death, winter and harvest, church and family traditions."*

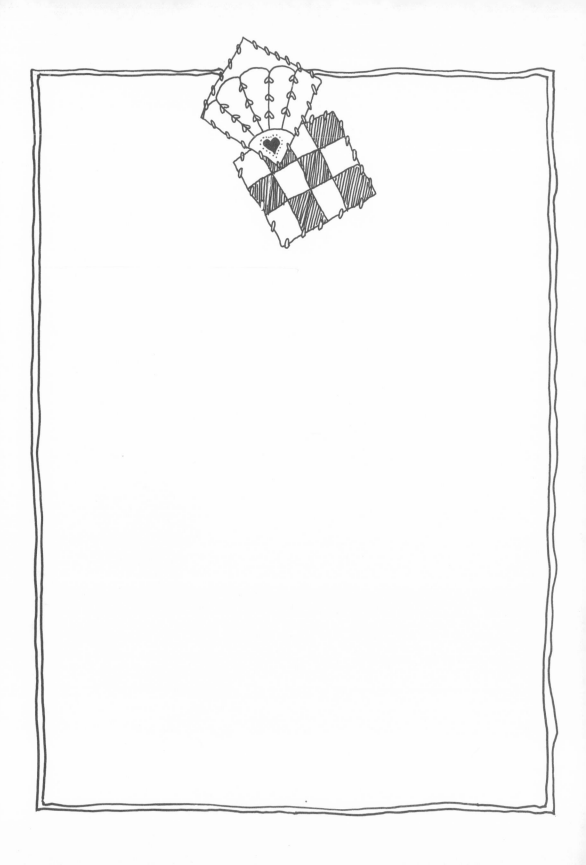

*"As I concentrate on quilting, the pieces of my frazzled life settle into focus."*

*"When I sleep under this crazy star quilt my grandmother made, I sometimes dream that I'm living in a sod house on the Oklahoma prairie."*

*"Quilting runs in the family. It's like a gene."*

*"When we were young, we used to take the baby blue and white nine-patch that Grandma made, drape it over the table like a tent, then hold private club meetings in our quilt-fort."*

*"I pieced the giant dahlia with the navy and burgundy after my grandmother died."*

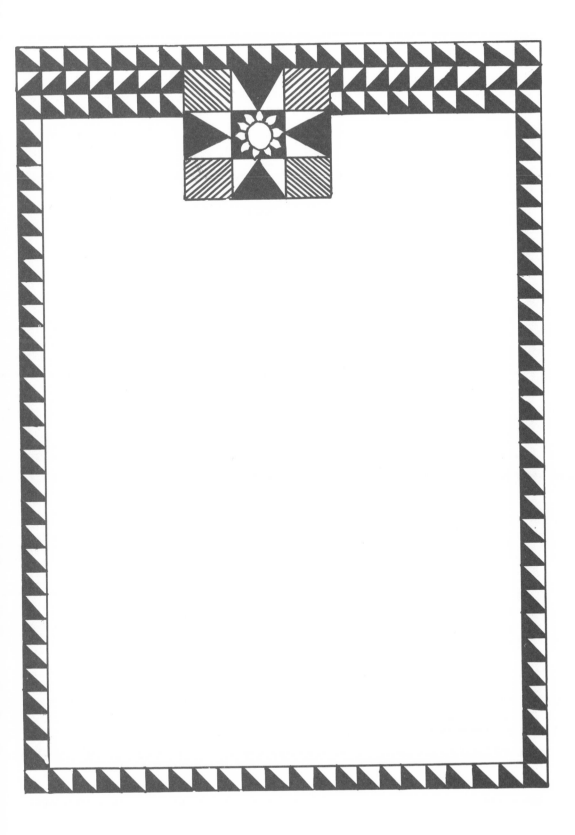

*"The children like to play with their toy cars on the bed. The sashes between the patches are roads and the patches are city blocks."*

*"New pattern ideas sometimes come out of nowhere. A flower garden or a rose arbor or the patterns on a patio suddenly pop out at you, your creative juices surge, and you make a dash for your needle and your fabric supplies."*

*"One year I made four quilts: a pink baskets pattern for spring, sunshine and shadow for summer, wild goose chase in the fall, and a white and blue bear paw for winter."*

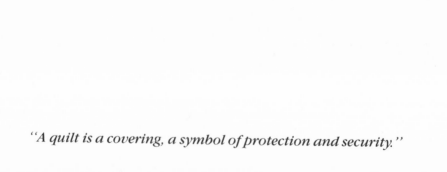

*"A quilt is a covering, a symbol of protection and security."*

*"My favorite spot to piece is by the window in the old oak rocker my grandfather made for my grandmother to sew in."*

*"Be a spontaneous quilter: put a surprise dash of color in an unexpected place; add some personal twist to a traditional pattern; play around with quilting designs."*

*"The lines of quilting on a plain quilt make me think of spider webs on dewy mornings."*

*"My grandmothers both lived hard lives. One became very quiet and sad and her quilts are full of rich, dark colors. The other made the best of her situation, and there's something bright in each of her quilts."*

*"A quilt is a work of art, like an oil painting or sculpture, and quilts too display something of the soul and being of their makers."*

*"On cold nights, my brother and I used to fight about whose turn it was to use the heavy comforter. It was a one-patch my mother had made out of drapery scraps for the top and a worn out cotton comforter for the batting."*

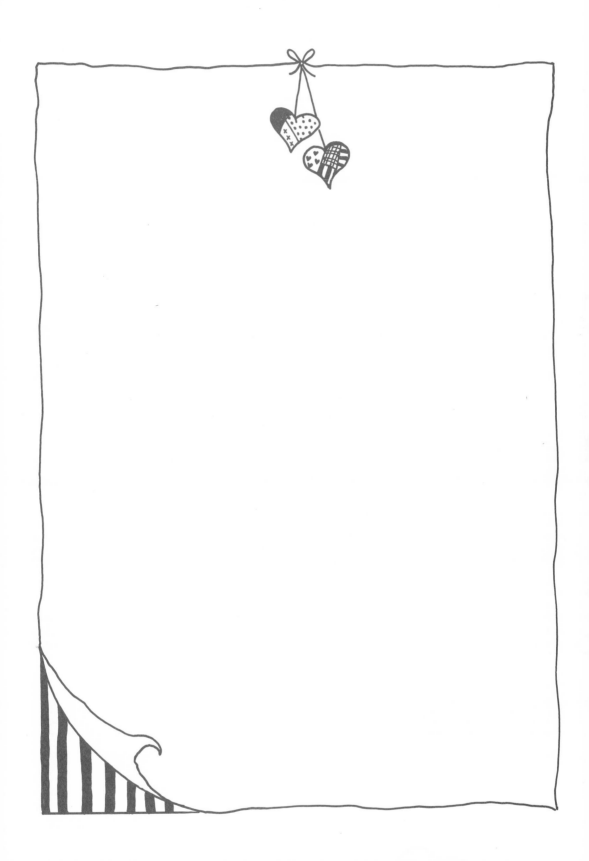

*"My people have always had a love for the earth—you can see it in the earthy colors of the quilts my grandmother made, and in the names of the quilts, like sunshine and shadow, lily, rail fence and bear paw."*

*"Quilting soothes me. Like a cup of hot lemon tea, or a cheery fire in the fireplace, it makes me feel at peace. I rest in it like a cat in a sunbeam."*

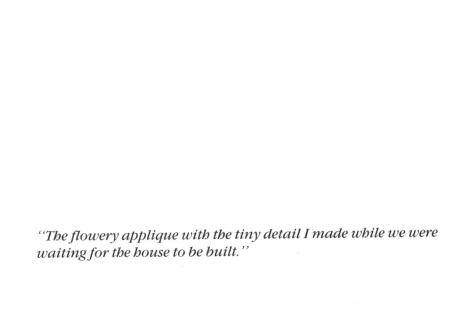

*"The flowery applique with the tiny detail I made while we were waiting for the house to be built."*

*"Give me some scissors, a pin cushion, thread and some fabric, and I'll be happy for hours."*

*"A friend of mine likes quilting so much, she searches auctions and sales for appliqued and pieced quilt tops, then quilts them."*

*"I like the random flashes of color in the ocean waves pattern with solid blocks between."*

*"As a child playing games of pretend, with grandmother's log cabin draped around my shoulders for my train. I was the noblest of rulers in our neighborhood kingdom."*

*"If a young woman makes a scrap quilt and doesn't use the same fabric more than once, it will bring her luck."*

*"Life cycles are hidden in the memories of our family quilts: newborns wrapped in their warmth, children huddling under their protective cover with thunder rumbling outside, grandparents covering chilly knees on breezy days."*

*"Quilts are our art, the way we express what we feel about life."*

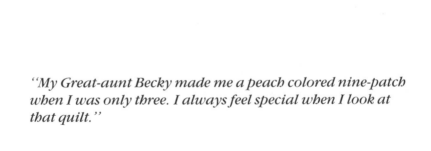

*"My Great-aunt Becky made me a peach colored nine-patch when I was only three. I always feel special when I look at that quilt."*

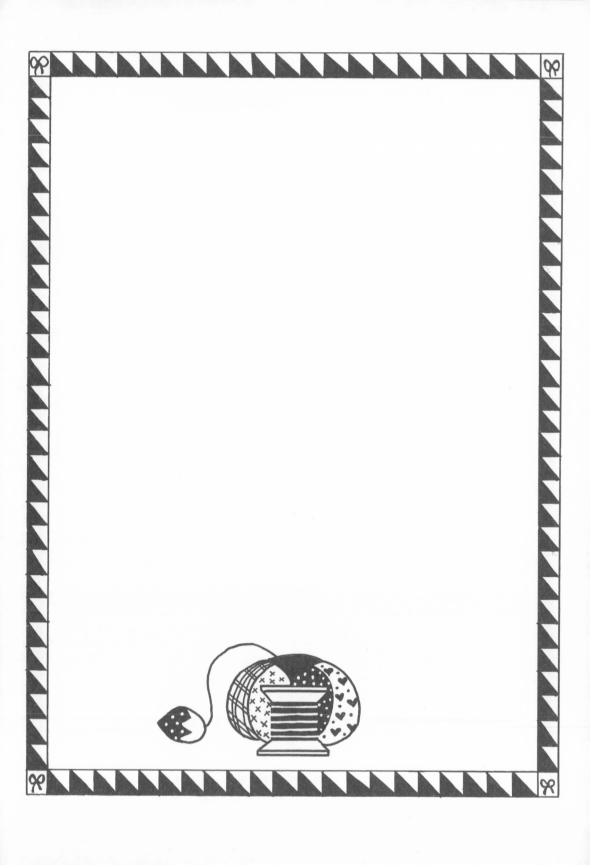

*"My favorite designs are the ones that play with your eyes, like the tumbling blocks and rail fences."*

*"Long ago the men farmed and the women quilted—straight, even rows of quilting like rows of corn, blocks of solid colors like planted fields, trees of life like the fat apple trees in the orchard."*

*"I started my first quilt when I was four, piecing bits of old feed sacks together."*

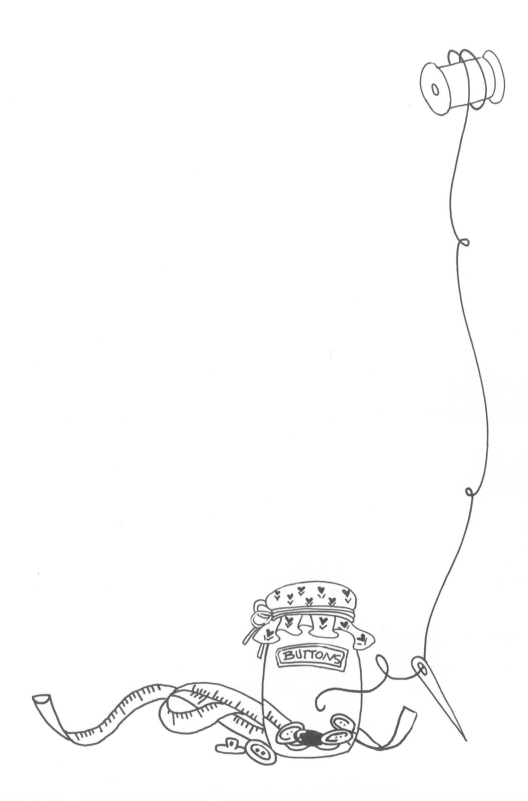

*"Something mysterious takes place in me when I sit down to quilt: I breathe more evenly and slowly, my pulse relaxes, my scattered thoughts fall into place."*

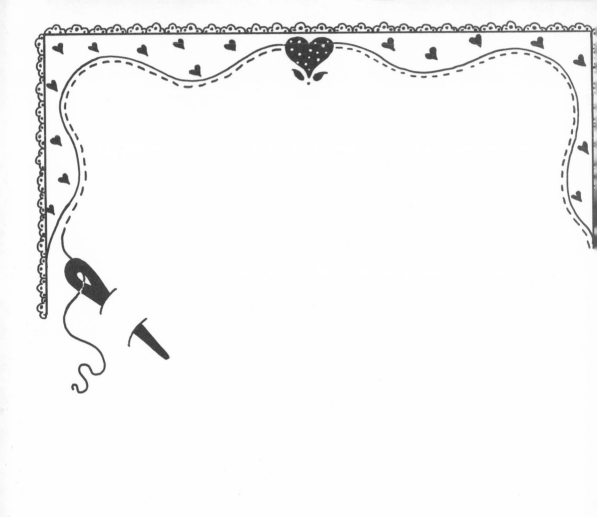

*"My great-grandmother, who couldn't read or write, recorded our family history with her needle and fabrics."*

*"I like the wild abandon of crazy quilts."*

*"Quilts piece memories together: the red calico print of my Sunday dress when I was a girl, the navy blue cotton plaid that Mother wore to committee meetings, the sunny yellow skirt I wore on my first day of high school."*

*"I made that star with the flourishes of yellow while I was expecting my first child."*

*"My most exciting designs often come from a few hours of pure piecing."*

*"My grandmother made us cousins keep tearing out our stitches until we got them perfect."*

*"I like to try new piecing and applique patterns, but I always seem to use feathers in my quilting."*

*"Even more special to me than our bed quilts is an old and tattered, brightly-colored crazy that we use for picnics and take on camping trips to keep warm while we toast marshmallows and sing campfire songs."*

*"Today we buy fabrics especially for making quilts. My mother used mostly scrap fabric in her quilts."*

*"Winters when I was a child saw a new quilt in our frame almost every other week."*

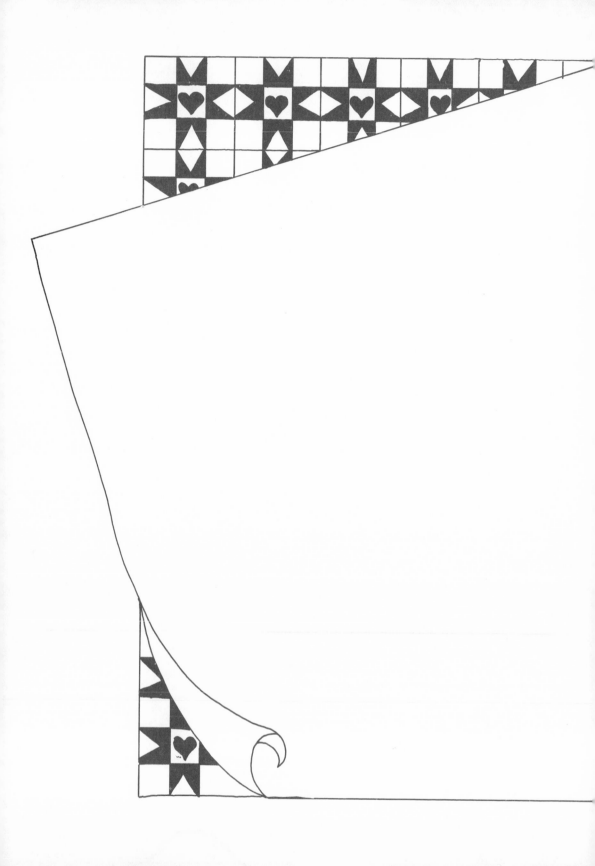

*"I always like to work a little purple into my quilts. It adds a bit of punch to them."*

*"Some days I'll sit down with a bag of scraps and begin to snip and piece without any idea where I'll end up."*

*"Women in the previous generations had less say about things than the men. They spoke their minds in the quilts they made and the colors and designs they chose."*

*"Quilt artists become very involved with their art medium, probably more than any other kind of artist. The feel of fabric is so important in quilt making."*

*"The way I feel about major experiences in my life goes into my quilts. That makes it hard for me to give them up."*

*"When you put certain colors beside each other, they blend together or set each other off. Color choice is the key to a good quilt."*

*"We always put some kind of mistake in our quilts—don't want to get too proud, you know."*